People Who Have Helped the World

SIR PETER SCOTT

by Julia Courtney

Picture Credits
Brian & Cherry Alexander, p. 48; Ardea, pp. 12-13, 50 (top); Bruce Coleman, p. 51 (both); Keystone Collection, pp. 35, 42; Oxford Scientific Films, p. 50 (bottom); Popperfoto, pp. 5, 6, 7 (both), 25; Press Association, cover; Teddy Schwarz Travel Trade Photo Library, p. 13; Sir Peter Scott personal archives, pp. 10, 11, 15, 17, 19, 21 (both), 26, 28, 56, 57; Philippa Scott, pp. 4, 9, 16, 20, 23, 30-31, 36, 40, 41, 44, 55 (both), 59; Ron Tavier Films, p. 37; The Wildfowl Trust, pp. 32, 33; World Wide Fund for Nature, p. 46.

The publishers owe special thanks to Philippa and Peter Scott for all their help and hospitality in the course of producing this book. We are particularly grateful for the loan of many personal and family photographs.

In addition, the publishers would like to thank all of Sir Peter's staff in Slimbridge for their help — especially Cassandra Phillips and June White. The publishers would also like to thank the Wildfowl Trust and World Wide Fund for Nature in London, Slimbridge, and Geneva for their generous assistance on this book.

The publishers wish to thank William Collins, Sons and Co. Ltd. (publishers of Sir Peter's *Travel Diaries of a Naturalist*) and Phaidon Press Ltd. (publishers of Sir Peter's *Observations of Wildlife*) for their generous permission to quote from these books.

North American edition first published in 1989 by
Gareth Stevens, Inc.
7317 West Green Tree Road
Milwaukee, WI 53223 USA

First published in the United Kingdom in 1988 with an original text © 1989 by Exley Publications Ltd.
Additional end matter © 1989 by Gareth Stevens, Inc.

Library of Congress Cataloging-in-Publication Data

Courtney, Julia.
    Sir Peter Scott.

    (People who have helped the world)
    "First published in the United Kingdom in 1988 with an original text by Exley Publications Ltd.
and Gareth Stevens Inc."--Verso t.p.
    Includes index.
    1. Scott, Peter Markham, Sir, 1909-   . 2. Naturalists--Great Britain--Biography.
I. Title. II. Series.
QH31.S36C68 1988   508'.092'4 [B]   88-2076
ISBN 1-55532-844-X
ISBN 1-55532-819-9 (lib. bdg.)

Series conceived and edited by Helen Exley
Picture research: Kate Duffy
Research: Diana Briscoe
Editorial: Margaret Montgomery
Series editor, U.S.: Rhoda Irene Sherwood
Editor, U.S.: Valerie Weber
Editorial assistant, U.S.: Scott Enk
Additional end matter, U.S.: Ric Hawthorne

Printed in Spain

1 2 3 4 5 6 7 8 9 94 93 92 91 90 89

SIR PETER SCOTT

Champion for the environment and founder of the World Wildlife Fund

by Julia Courtney

Gareth Stevens Publishing
Milwaukee

"An awful place"

The time: March 1912

The place: A frail tent amid the lonely wastes of Antarctica, 170 miles (274 km) from McMurdo Sound, Ross Island.

Outside, a blizzard howled as it had done for the past ten days; inside, a dying man struggled painfully to scrawl a farewell letter to the family he knew he would never see again.

Months earlier, Captain Robert Falcon Scott and his companions had set off, determined to be the first explorers ever to reach the South Pole, a great achievement for their country, Great Britain, and for the cause of scientific discovery. After a demanding journey, they had finally arrived at the Pole, only to find that a Norwegian group led by Roald Amundsen had gotten there just one month before. "Great God! This is an awful place!" recorded Scott in his diary before they began the interminable march of nine-hundred miles (1,440 km) back to McMurdo Sound.

Now the little party was overcome by tiredness, accidents, and dangerous weather conditions. Captain Scott watched his friends die bravely, knowing that he too had not long to live. It was time to send a last message home to his wife, Kathleen, and their son Peter, two-and-a-half years old.

Thinking of his young child, Captain Robert Falcon Scott wrote, "Make the boy interested in Natural History. It is better than games. . . . Make him a strenuous man." These words, and the circumstances in which they were written, were to have a tremendous influence on the life of that boy, who became the artist and naturalist, Peter Markham Scott.

Opposite: This picture of Adélie penguins in the Antarctic was photographed by Sir Peter's wife, Philippa Scott.

Below: Peter Scott's father, Captain Robert Falcon Scott, explorer of the Antarctic.

The naturalist who influenced a generation

Captain Scott could hardly have dreamed that his son was to be fascinated by nature his entire life and that Peter would grow up to change the way millions of people think about their environment.

But the World Wildlife Fund (WWF), now called the World Wide Fund for Nature, owes its existence largely to Peter. He stands out among the small group of people who "invented" nature conservation as an issue vital to a growing number of concerned people.

Thanks to these naturalists and conservationists, more of us are becoming aware of misguided actions. People in developed nations consume too many resources, and people in developing nations often plan poorly, so land, water, and other resources are used unwisely. Many nations cannot control their population growth, and the resources of these nations are sorely strained. We must learn to conserve, to live more intelligently within our world.

Peter Scott has helped us understand our actions. The story of how he has done this began in that lonely tent in the distant polar snows.

Peter Scott's mother, Kathleen Scott, with his famous father, Captain Robert Falcon Scott, who died when Peter was two-and-a-half. Captain Scott had asked Kathleen to encourage Peter to be interested in nature. She gave Peter a magical childhood, surrounded by people who cared about nature. He grew up with a passionate interest in all wild things.

Son of a famous father

Captain Scott's doomed expedition to the South Pole made him a national hero. When the bodies of the lost polar explorers were recovered some months later, Scott's diary was also found. Its tale of courage and endurance seized the imagination of the British public, and the memory of Captain Scott and his men was acknowledged throughout the land.

Young Peter Scott, born on September 14, 1909, grew up knowing that his father had been a brave and famous man. He was proud of his father's achievements, but he came to realize that to succeed in life, he would have to "strike out on a line of my own," as he put it. Fortunately his father's hope that he would be interested in nature allowed him to do just that.

Because Peter had lost his father so early — in fact, he never really knew him — it was especially fortunate that he had a remarkable mother. A talented professional sculptor, Kathleen Scott was able to encourage her son's artistic ability as well as his growing interest in nature.

In many ways, Peter was lucky. His family was not poor, and he could look forward to the traditional

Below left: On June 6, 1911, Captain Scott's birthday was celebrated with a party at Base Camp during his expedition to the South Pole. The festive meal was a welcome break from the demanding routine of scientific work in harsh conditions, and helped to keep the men cheerful and enthusiastic. Sadly, this was to be his last birthday, as he died in the early months of 1912.

Below right: Silhouetted against the Antarctic skyline is a huge wooden cross that honors the memory of Scott and his three companions.

education and advantages of an English gentleman of the time. Also, his lively mother was a friend of many famous and interesting people. She could also provide vacations in other countries (then a rare and unusual treat for most people) and the companionship of clever and knowledgeable adults.

His mother was ingenious in her response to his father's request that he study natural history, Peter later thought. "She did not thrust the subject down my throat, but instead put me most subtly into the way of naturalists and biologists of all kinds who were prepared to give time to me because of the passage in my father's letter." Two influential people who took a special interest in the boy were his godfathers, Sir Clements Markham and Sir James Barrie.

Admiral Sir Clements Markham, president of the Royal Geographical Society, was close to the Scott family. He inspired Captain Scott's expedition, and the Scotts used his name as Peter's middle name.

His other godfather was famous as J. M. Barrie, creator of *Peter Pan*. The celebrated playwright gave Peter a Life Fellowship in the Zoological Society of London, which meant that, among other privileges, he could go to the London Zoo whenever he wanted. When Peter was four, Barrie took him to a performance of *Peter Pan*. Peter later recalled that the high point of this outing came during the intermission, when he dropped his program over the balcony, scoring a direct hit on the head of a woman seated below.

Lizards, caterpillars, and geese

Although Peter and his mother lived in London and for a short time in Paris, they spent long holidays at Shingle End, a seaside cottage on the south coast of England. Here the boy discovered lizards hiding in the cracks at the bottom of an old wall, the first of many reptiles he was to study. He watched fascinated as caterpillars fed near the house.

At Shingle End he became aware of the sound and sight of birds, especially the skylark and sea birds such as waders and ducks. Once, a V-shaped group of Brent geese flew low over the sea. Peter did not then know what they were, but the sight impressed him deeply.

He soon realized that he had seen his first wild geese.

Peter spent active days exploring the seashore with his mother. He hunted for insects and frogs, observed birds, learned the names of common plants and flowers, and tried to draw everything he saw.

By the time he was ten, Peter was already, as he wrote, "deeply committed to Natural History." He learned a great deal about ornithology, the study of birds, and was soon able to identify many different species — although he was overly optimistic in listing as "rarities" some species he had spotted.

His enthusiasm for butterflies and moths led to a friendship with Evelyn Cheeseman, the Curator of Insects at the London Zoo. Soon the young artist had the thrill of seeing his drawing of a privet hawk moth caterpillar reproduced in one of her books on insects.

Already interested in boats, young Peter Scott poles a canoe, happy in the outdoor life.

Additions to the family

At about this time Peter acquired a stepfather, when his mother decided to marry Edward Hilton Young, known as Bill. Bill was immensely knowledgeable about birds, and Peter was delighted with his mother's choice. Later, another member was added to the family with the birth of Peter's half-brother, Wayland.

This was also a time of exciting travel, including a visit to Tunisia, in North Africa, where Peter learned to ride a camel.

A new enthusiasm for marine life led Peter's family to send him to a special course run by the Marine Biological Association at Plymouth, England. Searching for creatures in rock pools and under stones, Peter was amazed at the beauty of their delicate shapes and listened enthralled as the course leader explained the range of variation within a single species. As he explained later, for the first time the fourteen-year-old boy began to realize that "these species were the current end products of forty million centuries of evolution — four billion years. . . . One of the greatest fascinations in nature is the way that evolution has produced this diversity of species moulded by the particular environment they live in."

A new school

In 1923, Peter went to Oundle, a British boarding school. Kathleen and Bill chose this school because science was particularly well taught there. As one of England's great private schools, Oundle also prided itself on molding character.

Pupils were taught that their privileged position as wealthy and well-educated citizens involved responsibilities; as adults they would be expected to take the lead in society and to act for the good of all. This ideal sank deeply into Scott's mind, to surface later as the conviction that his job was to make the whole human community realize its responsibility for Earth.

Individualism and initiative were encouraged at Oundle, but even so, Peter's unconventional streak occasionally caused difficulties! The school was located near a river and freshwater fishing was a popular hobby among the boys. Scott soon became an expert

Peter, age thirteen, photographed with a friendly lizard. He was enthusiastic about reptiles, and when on vacation on the French island of Noirmoutier at the mouth of the Loire River, he wrote home proudly to tell his stepfather that he had discovered four different kinds of lizards.

angler and much preferred fishing to organized games, sometimes getting into trouble for missing soccer matches. The teachers also disapproved of his habit of keeping a pet ferret in his pocket.

Helped by a friend, Peter reared owls and bats and, of course, he had not lost his love of caterpillars. "Since school days I have had a great interest in hawk moths," he wrote in his book, *Observations of Wildlife*. "I always thought these were the best." More than forty years later, in 1969, on a visit to Qatar, he was delighted to find twelve caterpillars of the rare oleander hawk moth which he brought home. He believed that every child should begin the study of nature by becoming an expert on one particular animal or plant.

Wildfowl were yet another interest at Oundle. For the first time Scott encountered gray geese and learned to identify white-fronted, pink-footed, and Bean geese.

Cambridge University

Like this solitary hunter, Scott spent many nights searching for wildfowl on the Fens,"far from even the loneliest human habitation, out on the wild marshes and mud flats where they roost at night and whence they flight in to feed at dawn, silhouetted against the eastern sky."

After working hard in his final years at school, although he confessed that few academic awards came his way, Peter was accepted at Trinity College, Cambridge. He enjoyed the beautiful surroundings of one of Britain's oldest and greatest universities and quickly made new friends.

He was soon rather disappointed in the course he had chosen. His subject, natural sciences, meant the study of zoology (animals), botany (plants), physiology (the workings of the body) and geology (the history and structure of the Earth). In 1927, when Peter arrived at Cambridge, few people had any ideas about "the web of ecology," the way in which plants, animals, and even Earth's climate are all dependent on one another. In fact, it is partly due to Sir Peter Scott himself that we are aware of this today.

So Peter found himself restricted to a study of dead animals, which were much less interesting to him than live ones. "Anyone can learn the names of fossils and the classifications of animals, but I don't want to do things that anyone can do. Anyone can't paint — and

I suppose that's why I like it. . . . I suppose it's scope for imagination that I want and there isn't any that I can find in the inside of a dogfish," he complained.

The active Scott, who hated to be bored, went looking for more exciting adventures. Joining the University Cruising Club, he began to develop into an expert yachtsman. He also became one of the famous "Night Climbers of Cambridge," a group of daring students who pursued the perilous and strictly forbidden sport of roof climbing on the historic towers and pinnacles of the school. The climbs took place at night, which added to both the danger and the excitement. As a talented artist, Peter was able to illustrate the anonymous *Roof-climber's Guide to Trinity*.

His childhood interest in drawing led him to illustration, and he contributed pictures for a book called *Adventures Among Birds*. He was asked to draw portraits of prominent characters for the university magazine, *Granta*. His bird paintings began to appear in a national magazine, *Country Life*, and he held a successful exhibition of his paintings in a Cambridge bookstore. Only a few were not sold and Scott continued to exhibit there yearly.

Below: King's College, Cambridge, where Scott spent four years as a student. The high medieval pinnacles of the university proved a challenge for the Night Climbers.

Peter, the hunter

The inspiration for Peter's increasingly popular paintings was the most absorbing of his university interests — hunting wildfowl. He became enthusiastic about the hunting of ducks, geese, and snipe in the wild, desolate area of fens or bogs. The Cambridgeshire Fens are a low-lying marshy area, partially drained during the seventeenth and eighteenth centuries but basically unsuitable for building or agriculture.

The Fens were one of the few really wild parts of Britain. Scott was attracted by the unspoiled nature of the place and by the chance to observe wildlife — especially the waterfowl that had always fascinated him. For Peter and his companions, the main appeal of these outings was the sheer difficulty of stalking the waterfowl and the lure of the outdoors.

It seems surprising in light of Scott's later career as a conservationist that he spent so much of his time hunting wildfowl as a young man. Even in those days, when the morality of shooting animals for sport was rarely questioned, Peter was asked why someone with his obvious enjoyment of birds could enjoy trying to kill them. His answer was that he did not sentimentalize the ducks and geese he shot, but respected their wildness while meeting them in the primitive combat of hunter and hunted.

He also enjoyed the excitement of the chase in stalking deer. For the people Scott grew up with, the sports of hunting, shooting, and fishing were an accepted part of life.

A hunter was expected to observe rules that governed these activities — rules that, for instance, protected the birds and animals during their breeding seasons. So long as this was done, no harm was thought to result from the killing of wildlife.

Eventually Peter's own ideas were to change. He had always had a streak of unconventionality in his character and a staunch determination to make up his own mind about the things that mattered. But at this stage, when he was still a teenager, it was hard to separate his instinct to explore the wild and observe its inhabitants from the sort of country pursuits expected of him as an English gentleman.

Sir Peter himself also pointed out that his early hunting experiences trained him in the close observation of wildfowl in their natural habitat, developing his interest in their movements and habits.

A change to art

It was becoming obvious that Scott was unhappy with his university courses, and his anxious stepfather wrote to ask why he had missed so many lectures. Peter needed to think seriously about his future; he decided to change to a course on the history of art and architecture in order to become a professional artist.

He later wrote," I have never regretted this great and momentous decision, for at one sweeping my whole outlook on life was changed and enlarged." Having made this choice, he was able to work much harder during his fourth year, harder than he had in his first three. He was allowed to stay on at Cambridge to complete the extra work and succeeded in gaining a degree in 1930.

Scott changed his university major from science to art, and by his early twenties he was already a famous artist. Without his talent and his persistence in developing it, he would never have had the strong financial base for his future achievements on behalf of wild animals.

Scott aimed to "upgrade the standards of truth in bird painting" by accurately capturing the likeness of the species depicted. He would usually set the birds in a picturesque background.

A successful artist

Scott then spent a year in Munich, Germany, studying art and learning German. Returning to England, he spent another year studying art at the prestigious Royal Academy Schools in London. Then it was time to earn his living as a professional artist.

Feeling that his best work reflected his passion for wild geese and other waterfowl, he decided to spend the winter of 1933 living and painting at Borough Fen Decoy, near Peakirk, England.

About forty paintings, mostly in oils, resulted from Peter's winter at Borough Fen. Two had the distinction of being exhibited at the Royal Academy in London and almost all the rest were sold after appearing in a special one-man show.

A commission requested at this time led to the creation of one of Scott's most famous pictures. Asked to produce an oil painting measuring eight feet by five feet, he was so daunted by the thought of attempting anything so large that he put off starting until a few days before his client was due to see the painting. Helped by his mother, who filled in the background of tall reeds, Peter managed to finish in time. Not only was the buyer highly delighted, but the picture also appeared in Peter's book about wildfowl hunting, *Morning Flight*. As *Taking to Wing*, a romantic title that the artist would never have chosen for himself, hundreds of thousands of copies of the painting were sold and made Peter Scott a household name, with an assured sale for his work.

From now on Peter was able to support himself as an artist, and it remained his profession for the rest of his life. This profession would enable him to finance his conservation projects.

During his year studying art in Germany, Scott often missed his close contact with animals and tried to find time to visit the Bavarian countryside. Here he met this roe deer fawn. It was quite tame and settled in Peter's arms for a photograph.

Hunting — the change begins

By this time Peter's attitude toward shooting birds for sport had begun to change. Sir Peter Scott has been called "The Patron Saint of Conservation" and, like many "saints," he experienced something of a conversion in which his ideas underwent an important change.

In his autobiography, Sir Peter wrote of an incident in 1932 when he and a friend were shooting graylag geese. Two were wounded, and as he recalled, "as soon as we picked them up we hoped that they might not die. The birds which a few moments before we had been trying to kill, we were now trying to keep alive."

Happily, both geese recovered and lived for many years. They were not the last birds Peter Scott was to shoot, but from then on his interest lay more and more in the capture of live birds for observation and ringing. Scott began to study the techniques of netting wildfowl unhurt, and as part of this project, he went to live in an unused lighthouse.

Home at the lighthouse

Scott's new home was one of two small, ornamental lighthouses built at the end of the eighteenth century. East Lighthouse was a conical brick building with four floors, each consisting of one circular room. Peter decorated his bedroom in a pale green with white geese flying around the walls, and prepared another room for guests by fitting two beds suspended from the ceiling by stout ropes.

During the six years he lived there, he built several additions, including a studio for his painting. It was a wonderful base for an artist and naturalist, with extensive views over the Nene River on one side and the salt marsh and mud flats of the Wash sea inlet on the other.

Here Scott was able to build up a collection of live waterfowl. Twelve pink-footed geese were the nucleus of the group. Other geese and ducks were netted or arrived on his ponds of their own accord. Two great characters were pink-footed geese — Egbert, a young wild gander, and Anabel, a first-year bird who appeared at the lighthouse, having lost her family on the way from Iceland or Greenland. For the next two years, she joined the migrating flocks in May and returned to greet Peter in October.

Already, the young artist believed, as he was to explain much later, that it is important for each of us to get to know the personality of a particular animal, identifying with it and forming a bond of affection.

At this period of his life, Peter grew even more knowledgeable about wildfowl. He visited the United States, Canada, and Hungary and went as far afield as the Caspian Sea to find new species and to observe the migration patterns of wild geese. On one trip, he came home across Europe by train accompanied by three crates of wild geese. He ran out of money on the way, but he eventually arrived safely with his ruffled and hungry cargo.

"I tried to record something of the almost frightening intensity of my feeling for birds in wild places, and the way in which the sounds of the wild geese worked upon my emotions like the great "Sanctus" chorus of Bach's B Minor Mass."

Sir Peter Scott,
Morning Flight

A creative period

Scott's artistic career continued to be highly successful. He wrote and illustrated another book, *Wild Chorus*, and his annual exhibitions in London attracted many buyers for his paintings, including members of the British royal family.

Looking back, Peter felt that his painting improved technically at the lighthouse; his only problem was the difficulty of combining a more carefully detailed quality with the fresh, lively impression of sketches done from life. He chose to work with oil paints instead of watercolors and large canvases rather than small to escape his absorption in small detail that had affected his earlier work.

Scott realized that his best work was done quickly, in bursts of creative energy that often lasted well into the night. Now that he was an expert on waterfowl, which were his best-loved subjects, he was able to paint from memory and often worked on two or more canvases at once, letting the background of one dry while he completed the foreground of another.

Scott at East Lighthouse: "Long ago I decided that my home must always be within sight and sound of the winter wild geese." The lighthouse was surrounded on three sides by tidal pools where Scott fed the wild geese and ducks. Tame and unafraid, many would return each year to the safety and shelter of the lighthouse.

The British America's Cup challenger Sovereign. *As a top international yachtsman, Peter Scott put his intimate knowledge of wind and weather to good use. The triumphs and disappointments of his sailing career were crucial to him.*

Success at sea

Scott's other great interest at this time was sailing and here, as so often, he was magnificently successful. Already it was clear that while he was modest and unassuming, he was also adventurous, energetic, and able to turn his hand to almost anything. He owned a series of boats in which he competed in international events as well as races closer to home.

Perhaps the greatest thrill came in 1937, when on his fourth attempt, he won the Prince of Wales' Cup in his fourteen-foot sailing dinghy, *Thunder*. This was even more important to him than the bronze medal he had won at the Olympics in Germany for single-handed sailing in the previous year.

Service in World War II

But by the summer of 1939, when Peter was twenty-nine years old, everyone was becoming all too aware that Europe would soon be plunged into a war that would completely change the world. He later wrote: "It no longer seemed important to win a fourteen-foot dinghy race."

Scott's daring spirit ensured that he was not afraid of the prospect of conflict. But he knew that his happy, satisfying days at the lighthouse were over. He made arrangements for the care of his waterfowl before joining the Royal Naval Volunteer Supplementary Reserve, a special organization for yachtsmen who felt they had valuable skills to offer the wartime navy.

During World War II (1939-45), Scott served in the Royal Navy. After training, his first ship was the HMS *Broke*, a destroyer involved in the essential task of escorting convoys of merchant ships crossing the Atlantic Ocean.

Despite frequent boats of seasickness, Scott did well in the Navy. In 1940 he was promoted to First Lieutenant (second in command) and commended for bravery. At one point, German bombs almost sank Peter's ship, which was in the English Channel on its way to remove troops from France. Meanwhile, his inventive mind devised a camouflage scheme for a large proportion of the Atlantic fleet.

His own command

Soon Scott was given his own command, first of a new steam gunboat and then of his own small fleet, the Steam Gunboat Flotilla. He now had six boats under his control. In the spring of 1943, he won Britain's Distinguished Service Cross for his "skill in the handling of his force, and great determination in his engagement, pursuit and re-engagement of the enemy." Later that year, the steam gunboats were involved in what Sir Peter described as a brutal and desperate battle. And as Senior Officer, he earned an additional award for "well-judged and gallant action."

Active wartime service taught the sportsman and naturalist more valuable skills. He learned to organize, command, and delegate people and to make balanced, informed decisions. He would use these skills to the fullest in his conservation work in the future. If Peter had not survived the war, he would, of course, have been sadly missed by his family and friends. Perhaps he would have been remembered as a promising artist. But his most important work would never have been done. It was not until his return from the war that he was ready to begin life as a conservationist.

By the end of the war, Scott had a family of his own. He had married Jane Howard, who later became a well-known novelist. In 1943, their daughter, Nicola, was born. Absent for months on end during his naval career, at last he could spend time with his wife and child. Sadly, the Scotts' marriage was not to survive the stresses of war and separation. By the early 1950s they would part, although without bitterness.

Above: Scott on the bridge of the Gray Goose, *a Royal Navy gunboat patrolling the English Channel during World War II.*
Below: During the war, Scott continued to paint, but naval subjects replaced waterfowl. This is his first ship, the HMS Broke, *rescuing the crew of a merchant cruiser.*

A new life

What direction was his life to take, now that he was no longer a naval officer? After the war, he ran for Britain's Parliament but lost the election by 435 votes, a narrow margin. Scott then decided to return to painting and to the problems of preserving rare species of wildfowl; perhaps his peacetime work could usefully lie in these areas of conservation.

Scott also felt strongly that after the strains of the war years, he needed to return to his painting as well as to the study and observation of wildfowl. His love for wild geese was soon to lead to his first major conservation project and to a whole new way of life.

Before the war, Scott had kept a pair of lesser white-fronted geese in his collection of waterfowl at the lighthouse. At that time, this rare Arctic nesting goose had only once been recorded as a wild bird in Britain. Now a friend suggested that he should visit Slimbridge, a wild and beautiful site on the estuary of the Severn River where thousands of wild geese congregated for the winter. Perhaps he might be lucky enough to spot more specimens of these uncommon and beautiful birds.

The magic of Slimbridge

So on a chilly day in December 1945, when he was thirty-six years old, Scott and some companions arrived at Slimbridge. They forgot the cold and the mud as they spied overhead a great flock of Russian white-fronted geese. Flying within the flock were two lesser white-fronted geese and several pink-footed, Bean, barnacle, Brent, and graylag geese.

These, wrote Sir Peter, "brought the total number of kinds of wild geese we had seen together on that marsh to seven, and as we walked back . . . I came to the inescapable conclusion that this was the place in which anyone who loved wild geese must live. Here were two empty cottages which might become the headquarters of the research organization which had been taking shape in my mind over the war years, the headquarters of a new collection of waterfowl, of the scientific and educational effort which I believed was so badly needed for the conservation of wildfowl."

The Wildfowl Trust

This decision marked the beginning of the Wildfowl Trust, which would grow to save many species of rare birds and animals and to become one of Peter Scott's greatest contributions to conservation.

The trust was formed in November 1946. Slimbridge was an ideal situation for the headquarters of the new trust, with its unique grassy salt marsh, the

Opposite: After the war, Scott settled at Slimbridge, which was to become a permanent and beloved home. He would remain here for over forty years, and his work would be recognized as the single greatest contribution of any one person to the cause of the migrating birds of the world.

Scott produced this drawing as a symbol for the Wildfowl Trust, his first major conservation effort. Besides paintings in oils and watercolor, his artwork has included line drawings to illustrate books (especially identification manuals), letterheads, and designs for symbols, logos, medals, coins, and ties.

Dumbles, and a protecting bank of seawall that kept the tides back from the low-lying fields. From behind them, watchers could observe the geese unseen.

Four defensive wartime observation posts provided more cover for the ornithologists, and there was also a 100-year-old duck blind, like the one Scott had learned to use at Borough Fen.

A moment of truth

By now Peter himself seldom shot birds. Then the decisive moment came when he saw a goose with two broken legs stranded, unable to move, in an inaccessible part of the Severn estuary where he and his friends had been shooting.

For two days the goose could be seen, sitting on the mud, starving to death. Peter knew he could not reach it, either to help it or to put a quick end to its sufferings. He also knew that it might well have been one of his own shotgun pellets that had injured the bird.

For some time, Scott had felt less happy about shooting. Now he asked himself, "What right have we men to do this to a bird for our fun — to impose that kind of suffering? I should not want this for a sworn enemy and that goose was not my enemy when I shot at him — although I was his."

He went on to consider that, without being a bird, it was impossible to determine exactly what the goose was feeling. "But," he wrote, "in spite of all this the goose with the broken legs was upsetting."

Thus, Peter decided to sell his guns.

Happiness

From now on the development of Slimbridge as the site for the Wildfowl Trust absorbed much of Scott's boundless energy. Almost at once, work began: Observation huts were built, ponds were dug, and fences erected. At first, Peter lived in London, but then he moved into a tiny old cottage at Slimbridge. Living in this small cottage, he began to plan a home. It would have a large picture window that would overlook the landscaped lakes he had created.

Peter's work for the Wildfowl Trust was keeping

him busy, so busy that he needed an assistant. His first helper left to marry his half-brother, Wayland and, amazingly, history repeated itself when Peter decided to marry her replacement!

His second wife was Philippa Talbot-Ponsonby. A professional photographer, Philippa soon accompanied Peter on various expeditions, learning new skills, such as flying a plane or skin diving. "I'm travelling all over the world . . . together with a like-minded and wonderful wife," Sir Peter would say.

Philippa shared her husband's deep love of nature — except for caterpillars, as she recalled the squashy ones she had trodden on with bare feet during her South African childhood!

The couple were to have two children: Dafila, whose attractive name was the scientific name of one of the most elegant ducks, the pintail, and Richard Falcon, named after Peter's father.

Under Peter's cheerful and energetic exterior, the deeper feelings that brought him an almost mystic communion with his beloved wild geese were now able to find satisfaction in an extraordinarily happy family life.

A happy family occasion: Dafila Kathleen Scott is christened in the ship's bell of her grandfather's ship Discovery. *Here Dafila is admired by her proud parents and her half-sister Nicola, who had also been christened aboard the vessel.*

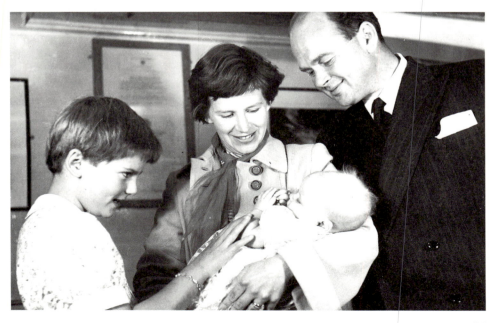

Ideals and achievements

From the beginning, one of the Wildfowl Trust's major objectives was the breeding of endangered species in captivity, with the goal being to return individual members of the species to the wild. The story of the Hawaiian goose, or nene, is a model early example of this work. Peter had been interested in the beautiful nenes since the 1930s. His plans to help the species had been interrupted by the war, and he was dismayed to hear that by 1950, the total number of nenes had dwindled to under fifty.

"The prospect of the extinction of any existing species is a potential disaster which man's conscience should urge him to prevent," announced Scott, and when his appeal to the government of Hawaii remained unanswered, he enlisted the help of a U.S. scientist who was working in the area.

Later, the curator of the Wildfowl Trust visited a Hawaiian man who, before World War II, had offered

Scott a pair of nenes from his garden. The curator returned with what he was told were a male and a female nene.

The birds settled down happily at Slimbridge. Both built nests; both laid eggs — infertile eggs. Clearly, the "pair" was in fact two females! Peter made a tiny hole in the shells, emptied the contents, made a tasty omelet, and preserved the shells.

He also sent an urgent telegram to Hawaii, and in due course a fine male nene arrived at Slimbridge. In his autobiography, Sir Peter recalled that the gander was named Kamehameha, after the greatest king of Hawaii, and his two mates were named Kaiulani and Emma, after famous Hawaiian royal women.

The following year, Kaiulani and Emma nested and reared nine young geese. By 1979, the world population of Hawaiian geese had risen to over twelve hundred. Peter sent two hundred back to Hawaii to re-establish the native nene population.

Rescuing birds from extinction

This was only the first of the Wildfowl Trust's rescue projects. The white-winged wood duck was once common in the tropical rain forests of Southeast Asia, its ghostly wail announcing its evening flight to feed on the waterweeds, seeds, small fish, and reptiles of the shaded forest pools.

Deforestation was already threatening this large perching duck when a group of Indian tea planters decided to send six pairs of birds from Assam, India, to Slimbridge to set up a breeding and reintroduction project. Special nesting boxes, lined with soil or peat, were designed to remind the birds of their usual nesting holes in tree trunks. Eggs were soon laid.

Raising the young birds proved more difficult, and it would take nearly twenty years before the white-winged wood duck was well established in captivity, with a colony of two hundred birds. The second phase of the operation could then begin with establishing breeding sites in Thailand and northeast India. From these, the birds could be gradually released into newly protected forest reserves.

Meanwhile, far from the Asian forests, Hungarian

"In northern Europe, some lakes are so polluted by acid rain that they are like vinegar."

From a brochure published by the World Wide Fund for Nature

27

Skillfully, Peter Scott untangles wild geese from one of the nets he invented to catch the birds unharmed. In this way, he catches and rings wild geese so that he can log their movements. Early work at Slimbridge included valuable studies of the breeding and migrations of Ross's snow geese and pink-footed geese. Years of painstaking work would enable the Wildfowl Trust to protect the migration paths of wildfowl and to save whole species.

naturalists were cooperating with the Wildfowl Trust in reintroducing the rare white-headed duck to the open, sandy plains and salt lakes of the Hungarian steppe. Fifty large, thick-shelled eggs, packed carefully into a portable incubator and watched over by staff from Slimbridge, were flown to Hungary.

That year twenty-seven young birds were successfully reared by hand in the Hungarian Kiskunsag National Park. Each subsequent year, offspring from these first birds have been reared in the safety of a controlled enclosure and then released back to their natural wild habitat to live and breed on their own.

International projects

Ornithologists all over the world were becoming involved in the work of the Wildfowl Trust. This international cooperation led to the foundation of the

IWRB, the International Waterfowl Research Bureau, now the International Waterfowl and Wetlands Research Bureau. This group, headquartered at Slimbridge, continues to do valuable conservation work.

The nene geese, the white-winged wood duck, and the white-headed duck were lucky. Scott and the Wildfowl Trust had intervened in time to save them from extinction.

But for other species it was already too late; Peter feared that the ivory-billed woodpecker, the pink-headed duck of India, and many other birds may have gone for good. He said sadly, "Extinction is forever. . . . Sometimes you have to play God; there's only so much money, so you've got to decide which species you're going to send it to help."

Mr. and Mrs. Noah

The preservation of endangered species like the nene goose is only one aspect of the work of the Wildfowl Trust. Another objective has always been the protection and study of migratory birds, again an area where international cooperation is vital. Here Peter's close involvement with the movements of wild Arctic swans was another magical story.

Bewick's swans, named after Thomas Bewick, the great nineteenth-century ornithologist and wood engraver, are fascinating. They live for about thirty years, always with the same mate. They can fly up to fifty miles (eighty km) an hour and cover vast distances during their migration. During the Arctic summer, these tundra swans, as they are called by the Soviets, breed in the lakes and marshes of northern Russia, but when the frosts come, they set out on the journey to their winter haunts two-thousand miles (3,200 km) away, in western Europe and Great Britain.

It was in 1948 that a stray Bewick's swan appeared at Slimbridge, probably attracted by tame North American whistling swans on the grounds. This first Bewick's swan was captured and paired with a mate provided by the Rotterdam Zoo. This pair was named "Mr. and Mrs. Noah" because they attracted a number of other Bewick's swans who wintered on a specially enlarged pool at Slimbridge.

Philippa's photograph of Bewick's swans on Swan Lake. This view from the huge studio window delights the Scotts and their friends. The scene is equally beautiful after dark, when the pond is floodlit to highlight the swans' white plumage against the dark water.

Swan Lake

Increasing numbers of swans began to arrive as Scott brought the tame Bewick's swans and others to Swan Lake. One swan settled in front of the picture window — and then many more came. Eventually, over three hundred wintered with the Scotts, bringing their cygnets (young swans) in mid-October, and setting out again for their breeding grounds by the end of March.

In his autobiography Peter wrote, "That these birds

should be drawn back after their five-thousand mile round trip to this tiny pond lying close under the walls of my house, gives me a feeling of wonder and delight that is hard to describe."

Before long, Peter made use of the discovery that each swan could be differentiated as an individual. He was able to tell them apart because the black and yellow pattern on each swan's bill was unique, like fingerprints in humans. Sir Peter compiled a dossier

Whooper swan migration route

 Bewick's swan migration route

 Whooper swan breeding range

Bewick's swan breeding range

of "mug shots," drawings of every swan to visit Slimbridge since 1964, complete with names.

Following the swans

How wild birds navigate has always been something of a mystery. They have been shown to use the sun, moon, and stars, but the exact speeds and heights at which they usually fly are difficult to determine.

It was to advance the study of Bewick's swans in their remote breeding habitat that in 1978 Sir Peter, with his wife and daughter, Dafila, made a short expedition to the Siberian Arctic. It was frigid but they were able to find and photograph swans' nests.

Painstaking research

The Scotts had been studying groups of swans and individual swans for over twenty years. They learned that one species, the Bewick's swans, found in the far

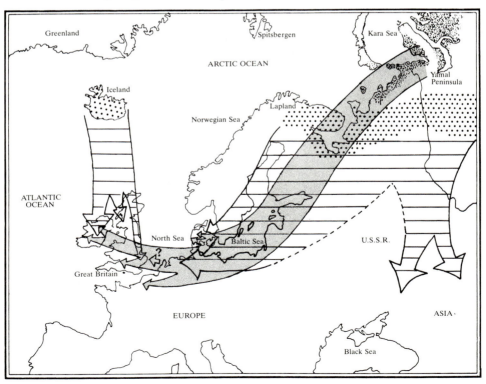

north as well as more temperate areas, lives for many years. This has allowed the Scotts to explore the way these swans migrate, the family relationships they form, and how they move about within areas.

As Scott remarked, they have learned "how important it is for the members of a pair to stay together for life in order to give them the best chance of breeding in the harsh arctic environment."

Wild geese

Peter had, of course, not lost his love of wild geese. Their welfare was important to the Wildfowl Trust, which he had founded to further the interests of all waterfowl.

To make possible the ringing of large numbers of wild geese, he invented a system of rocket-propelled nets to catch the birds unharmed. He visited the summer breeding grounds of both Ross's snow geese in the Arctic and in Canada and the pink-footed geese in the central highlands of Iceland.

The pink-footed geese were the subject of a particular inquiry in the 1950s. Scott later wrote, "We have marked more than 25,000 pinkfeet in ten years." This greatly increased their knowledge of this bird's migration and breeding patterns.

Education at Slimbridge

Yet another task of the Wildfowl Trust has always been to bring home the joys and responsibilities of conservation to the public. At the time, this idea was something relatively new. Before Peter's venture, the study of wildlife was mainly for a minority — for those with enough money and leisure to indulge in a demanding but fulfilling hobby and for some people who lived in the country, with ready access to birds.

From the beginning, the blinds and observation posts at Slimbridge were made comfortable and easily accessible. School parties, the elderly, and the disabled are always welcome. From the earliest days, there were always tales of how Sir Peter found time to greet visitors personally and to answer endless questions about wildlife.

Individual whooper or Bewick's swans can be identified by variations in their black and yellow bill markings. These usually fall within the three main types shown here: "Yellowneb," "Penny-face," and "Darky."

33

In addition to detailed information about the many species of wildfowl to be seen, Scott decided to convey some wider thoughts on world ecology. Setting up a permanent exhibition in 1966, he put up a mirror. Above it a notice read, "You are looking at a specimen of the most dangerous and destructive animal the world has ever known." He continued below, "He is also the most imaginative and creative animal, and has evolved a conscience — keep it with you as you go round this exhibition." Then came warnings of what Scott believed to be the three greatest dangers to humanity: nuclear war, overpopulation, and boredom in the Age of Leisure.

Over the years, the Wildfowl Trust has expanded. At Slimbridge, the original seventeen acres (seven hectares) has spread to over one-hundred acres (forty hectares) of pens, pools, and blinds, with another eight-hundred acres (320 hectares) of land for the winter flocks of wild Bewick's swans, wild white-fronted geese, and some thousands of wild ducks. There are also now seven other reserves in England, Wales, and Scotland, comprising a total of over three-thousand acres (1,200 hectares) visited by half a million people each year.

Looking ahead

On the fortieth anniversary of the founding of the Wildfowl Trust, Peter was characteristically unwilling to sit back and congratulate himself. Instead, he voiced what he thought should be the trust's ongoing work. Its purpose was to preserve wildfowl and their wetland habitat and to teach people about their importance. Because changes in farming techniques in the future could prove harmful to the wildfowl and their homes, it was essential for the research of the trust to continue and expand. As Scott said, "Many questions remain unanswered and no doubt, an even greater number are still unasked."

Peter felt that pure research by itself was important — anything we can learn about birds and their wetlands is useful. But we must apply the findings of pure research to be sure that the wildfowl flourish and increase in the future.

The Wildfowl Trust was Peter's first conservation effort, and it has always remained closest to his heart. It helped teach him the valuable truth that in order to preserve wildlife, conservationists must also preserve the environment. Migratory birds are globetrotters and need the ornithological equivalents of service stations, so the wetlands where they rest and refuel are vital for their survival.

Thanks largely to Peter Scott's dedication, this idea was brought home to naturalists all over the world. In 1971, a treaty was signed at Ramsar, in Iran. Forty participating countries eventually promised to care for their wetlands — marsh, fen, peat land, and water — especially as habitats for wildfowl of all kinds.

By 1988 there were 403 Ramsar sites in forty-eight countries. An area of seventy-four million acres (thirty-million hectares) had been pledged.

The gliding and sailing champion

Although absorbed in the Wildfowl Trust and many other activities, Peter continued with competitive sports. He learned a new skill, gliding, beginning at the age of forty-six. At first he saw gliding merely as an interesting hobby. But soon he was collecting certificates and awards and in 1963 experienced what he calls "one of the golden moments of my life" when he became British National Gliding Champion.

Despite the appeal of flying high-speed gliders, Peter did not lose touch with the world of sailing. To add to his previous triumphs in 1937 and 1938, he'd won the Prince of Wales' Cup for the third time, in 1946, the year after the war ended. From 1955 to 1969, he was president of the International Yacht Racing Union. In 1964 he was at the helm of *Sovereign*, the unsuccessful British challenger for the America's Cup. The loss, perhaps unfortunately, has stayed with him for years.

Failure and disappointment are rare occurrences for Peter Scott. It has been hard for him to come to terms with being second — this "terrible failure," as he described it. That he has regretted this experience for years perhaps shows something of the driving will to succeed hidden by his genuinely modest manner.

British Air Scouts and Rangers listen attentively as Peter Scott demonstrates the controls of a glider. He had taken up the sport as a possible alternative to sailing, because he had little time for long journeys to the coast where he sailed. He soon became fascinated by the skills and thrills of gliding. The knowledge of winds and air currents gained as a sailor and a wildfowl expert helped him excel at this sport.

A new world

It was his connections with television and with sailing that led indirectly to his participation in yet another sport and to the discovery of a whole new world of nature study. In 1956, Peter, as president of the International Yacht Racing Union, was on his way to the Olympic Games in Melbourne, Australia, at the same time taking the opportunity to film wildlife for a documentary on Australia.

During a three-day visit to the Queensland coast, Peter and Philippa went swimming with face masks and snorkels around the Great Barrier Reef. "Nothing I have done in Natural History in all my life has stirred me quite so sharply as my first experience of skin-diving on a coral reef. . . . The dramatic threshold which is crossed as soon as one puts one's mask below the surface is, to a naturalist, nothing less than stagger-ing in its impact."

He continued, "Much has already been written about the scarcely explored new 'continent' of the ocean; I have read these descriptions . . . and yet I was unprepared for the visionary revelation when I first saw the real thing."

In his autobiography, Peter wrote, "My diary is full of drawings of fish — the common fishes of the coral reef. I drew the marvellous yellow and black striped and barred Butterfly Fish of the genus *Chaetodon*. I drew the black and white Damsel Fish, . . . the superb Anemone Fish . . . which are golden-red with pale blue bands, and the ridiculous Razor Fish which swim perpetually standing on their heads. But to begin with I did not know their names."

Peter's ignorance was short-lived. He was soon pondering many questions about the habitats and habits of fish. He went on to learn scuba diving in the Bahamas and dove to study fish in the Indian Ocean, the Red Sea, the Arctic, the Antarctic, the Caribbean, and the West, South, and Central Pacific. Before long, Philippa Scott shared her husband's enthusiasm — they were both "thrilled to bits" when in 1988, "a beautiful little fish" from the Coral Sea was named *Cirrhilabrus scottorum* after them, in recognition of their contribution to nature conservation.

Above: This angel fish painting is one of the set of jewel-like works Scott completed after a visit to the Wingate Reef. Here in the Red Sea, the water was clear, the corals were brilliant, "the fishes were absolutely fabulous," Scott wrote. Enchanted by the area, he and Philippa used their fame and influence to support the conservationists who were fighting for the world's coral reefs.

Opposite: Scott off Heron Island in Australia's Great Barrier Reef. This area first awakened the Scotts' interest in snorkel-ing. Over the years they have built up records of the diverse species in different reefs. One fish they discovered was named after them.

Coral reefs

Although we can easily understand the threat to birds and mammals through our hunting and destroying of their habitats, the danger facing the world's coral reefs is not so obvious. Over the years, however, Peter Scott and other conservationists began to realize that the mounting destruction of coral reefs was posing a serious problem. These reefs are an important part of the web of ecology, and their disappearance would be a disaster for humanity and wildlife alike.

Coral reefs are useful in several ways: They provide homes for fish, mollusks, and crustaceans, and they act as breeding grounds for the young of edible fish. They also protect coastlines against waves and storms, forming beaches and sheltered havens. As tourist attractions, they help local vacation areas, and they have great scientific and education value for researchers and students. Coral is also used for jewelry. All in all, the reefs are essential systems that must be conserved and managed so that legitimate use (for example, for fishing) does not threaten their long-term survival and growth.

Unfortunately, a number of problems face the reefs. A major threat is "siltation," the situation that arises when people do not plant their land well and soil erodes. The eroded soil, called silt, runs into the rivers and then reaches the sea, where it can smother and kill the coral.

Another obvious problem is oil pollution, which occurs when oil tankers or oil rigs break, releasing thousands of barrels of oil into the sea. A third kind of pollution, the pouring of thousands of gallons of untreated liquid and solid waste into the sea, leads to the growth of coral-damaging algae.

At the same time, the desire for more industries tempts communities to remove large sections of the reefs, either in the process of improving the harbors or in using the reefs for commercial enterprises, such as cement making. People who exploit the reef and use poor fishing methods deplete the marine life that grows there. Finally there is nuclear testing, particularly in the Pacific Ocean, which could threaten the entire ecosystem.

Peter as a communicator

The formation of the Wildfowl Trust was not Peter Scott's only chance to publicize natural history. He was becoming a well-known radio personality, first as the commentator for the World War II Victory Procession in London, and later for the royal wedding of Princess Elizabeth (now Queen Elizabeth II) to Philip, the Duke of Edinburgh. He also became a member of a popular children's radio series, "Nature Parliament," which was broadcast monthly for twenty years.

With the coming of television, he became the host of "Look," a British television series that featured natural history subjects with filmed sequences. Beginning in 1953, this was one of the first of many nature documentaries, and it won him Britain's Television Society Award in 1955. Later, for many years, Scott supplied commentaries for another pioneering nature series on British television, "Survival."

Scott's combination of expert knowledge and a pleasant, likable personality made him a popular figure, and his contributions made a considerable impact on media attitudes toward nature. One reason that Britain's television network, the British Broadcasting Corporation, chose to set up its unique Natural History Unit at Bristol was because both Peter and Slimbridge were nearby!

Global problems and global solutions

As Scott wrote in his book *Observations of Wildlife*, "My biological training told me that an environmental crisis was on its way. It was becoming abundantly clear that all was not well with Planet Earth."

After reading Rachel Carson's book, *Silent Spring*, and meeting the author, Peter wrote, "I found myself thinking more ecologically and environmentally. The science of ecology had not been invented when I was learning biology; yet the instant its principles were enumerated, I immediately realized the essential truth, that all nature is interrelated, that we are a part of it, and need contact with it. Furthermore, because we are, as a species, the direct cause of so much of the environmental damage, we have a clear responsibility."

Sir Peter chats with Britain's Prince Philip, Duke of Edinburgh, at one of many formal occasions. Conferences, dinners, and award ceremonies absorb much of Sir Peter's time but give him new opportunities to publicize the work of both WWF and the Wildfowl Trust.

This watercolor of a sable antelope comes from one of Scott's travel diaries. It was made on one of his many conservation trips. He has filled over forty diaries with detailed notes and sketches. Many are used as references for his oil paintings. Selections from the diaries have been published as his three-part Travel Diaries of a Naturalist.

As he began to consider nature on a global scale, Scott was becoming deeply involved in the work of the Swiss-based International Union for the Conservation of Nature and Natural Resources (IUCN). From the 1950s on, he had been a member of the IUCN's Survival Service Commission, which he chaired from 1962 to 1980. One of his major achievements there was the institution of the famous Red Data Books.

The Red Data Books

The IUCN's Survival Service Commission, now the Species Survival Commission, had clearly stated aims: "The prevention of the extinction of species, sub-species and discrete populations, thereby maintaining genetic diversity."

In other words, it was pledged to preserve any form of natural life that seemed to be in danger of dying out. But first, of course, endangered species needed to be identified while there was still time to take action.

Peter explains: "We began to list the species in danger in a series of loose-leaf books called the Red Data Books. We produced a volume for Mammals, another for Birds, one for Reptiles and Amphibia, and one for Fish — so that all the vertebrate animals have been covered. Now we are embarking on inverte-brates and on plants.

"The degree of threat has been colour coded — the most endangered on red sheets, those rare but not in immediate danger on white sheets, those still numer-ous but greatly depleted on yellow sheets (amber for caution), those about which we know too little on grey sheets (grey areas), and those formerly in danger but now out of danger on green sheets.

"It could be said that the object of the exercise is to get all the animals in the Red Data Books onto green sheets. Then we could wind up the whole operation."

Listing the endangered species is the first stage. The commission still has to find out why they are threatened, see what can be done, and then persuade people to do whatever is necessary to help. Thus, the commission has two programs. The first explores what should be done to stop the decline of a species. The second looks at how this can be accomplished.

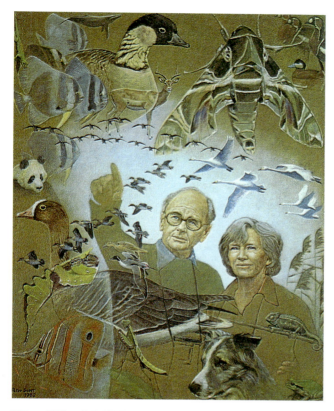

The World Wildlife Fund is launched

Clearly the IUCN had a lot of work to do. But Peter soon realized that this important international body had a major handicap — lack of money. One day in 1961, Peter came back from Morges, Switzerland, where he had been attending an IUCN meeting. Flying with him was Max Nicholson, at that time head of the British government's Nature Conservancy.

As the two men discussed the rather fruitless discussions of the past two-and-a-half days, during which a panel of distinguished scientists had been forced to spend their time worrying about how to pay for the next month's secretarial help, they felt that this situation could not continue. What was needed was a fully professional organization to raise money for conservation projects all over the world.

Peter — respected, unassuming, and persuasive —

"[Studying nature] leads me to value each evolutionary creation, each species, very highly, and to look upon species extinction at the hands of unthinking man — sometimes even by his deliberate choice — as wicked irresponsibility. Extinction is forever."

Sir Peter Scott,
Observations of Wildlife

contacted many eminent conservationists, including Professor Julian Huxley, the world-famous biologist, author, and educator.

An important element in the success of the World Wildlife Fund was Peter's ability to involve celebrated people in its work. The British royal family, for example, had been interested in Peter Scott for most of his life. Peter had stayed with King George VI at the royal family's country homes, and there were several royal visits to Slimbridge.

Peter Scott had high hopes of support from the royal family in this new venture, and later he recalled how he managed to recruit both Prince Philip, Duke of Edinburgh, and Prince Bernhard of the Netherlands on the same day.

Hearing that the Duke of Edinburgh was out of action with a painful leg, Peter approached him during

Watched by a group of young WWF supporters, Scott puts the finishing touches on the famous panda logo. He designed the symbol himself, choosing the much-loved but endangered panda partly because its black and white markings are easy to recognize. The design is also easy to create and to reproduce.

a physiotherapy session. The Duke agreed to become president of the British National Appeal. The new president, who over the years was to give tremendous impetus to WWF, then sent Scott off to an informal meeting with Prince Bernhard, soon to be the First International President of WWF.

The Prince of Wales, who is an ardent conservationist, has also given support whenever he can. Later, as president of the Wildfowl Trust, Prince Charles was often able to bring his children on informal trips to see the Slimbridge birds and the Scotts.

Scott himself was an active Chairman of Trustees of both the international body and the British National Appeal of the WWF. Because of his fame as an artist, writer, and broadcaster, Peter soon became identified with WWF in the public eye. But he has always pointed out that other eminent, if less well known, people were also closely involved.

One wise move in the beginning was getting the support of Guy Mountfort, an ornithologist and, importantly, a leading advertising agent. As an advertising agent, Mountfort has known how to make the goals of the group known to the world at large. As the 1986 Director's Review of WWF-UK reminded supporters, "WWF-UK is a professional organization, run on a business-like basis."

> *"We need people to make a personal contribution by taking responsible attitudes towards nature in their daily lives."*
> Prince Philip

The conservation creed

As a founder and first Chairman of WWF, Peter Scott was rapidly becoming the world's best-known conservationist. He expresses his beliefs concisely in what he called his "conservation creed." Here it is, a passionate statement of Peter Scott's deepest convictions:

"What man did to the Dodo, and has since been doing to the Blue Whale, and about 1,000 other kinds of animals, may or may not be morally wrong. But the conservation of nature is most important because of what nature does for man.

"I believe something goes wrong with man when he cuts himself off from the natural world. I think he knows it, [so] he keeps gardens and window-boxes and house plants, and dogs and cats and budgerigars.

"Man does not live by bread alone. I believe he

The Natural World of Man, *one of Scott's rare symbolic paintings. It represents the dilemma of our relationship with nature. The pointed end shows our responsibility to save animals facing extinction. From there the scope widens to include communities of animals and their relationship to the environment. The triangle then portrays soil erosion, industries, and overpopulation and the problems and pollution that they produce. With one white and one black hand, the human stands frozen before this terrifying pyramid of problems.*

should take just as great pains to look after the natural treasures which inspire him as he does to preserve his man-made treasures in art galleries and museums. This is a responsibility we have to future generations, just as we are responsible for the safe-guarding of Westminster Abbey or the Mona Lisa.

"It has been argued that if the human population of the world continues to increase at its present rate, there will soon be no room for either wildlife or wild places, so why waste time, effort and money trying to conserve them now?

"But I believe that sooner or later man will learn to limit his own overpopulation. Then he will become much more widely concerned with optimum rather than maximum, quality rather than quantity, and will rediscover the need within himself for contact with wilderness and wild nature.

"No one can tell when this will happen. I am concerned that when it does, breeding stocks of wild

animals and plants should still exist, preserved perhaps mainly in nature reserves and national parks, even in zoos and botanical gardens, from which to repopulate the natural environment man will then wish to re-create and rehabilitate.

"These are my reasons for believing passionately in the conservation of nature.

"All this calls for action of three kinds: more research in ecology, the setting aside of more land as effectively inviolate strongholds, and above all education. By calling attention to the plight of the world's wildlife, and by encouraging people to enrich their lives by the enjoyment of nature, it may be possible to accelerate both the change in outlook and the necessary action. . . .

"Much money is needed for relieving human suffering, but some is also needed for human fulfillment and inspiration. Conservation, like education and art, claims some proportion of the money we give to help others, including the as yet unborn.

"Even if I am wrong about the long-term prospects — if man were to fail to solve his own overpopulation problem, and reaches the stage . . . when there will be standing room only on this earth — even then the conservation effort will have been worth while.

"It will have retained, at least for a time, some of the natural wonders. Measured in man-hours of enjoyment and inspiration this alone would be worth the effort. Many will have enjoyed the pictures even if the gallery is burnt down in the end.

"The community chest which seeks to make the gallery representative and maintains the fire-alarm system is the World Wildlife Fund."

Early years of WWF

At first, WWF moved forward slowly. Nevertheless, during its first five years, 1961 to 1966, almost three million dollars were directed into conservation.

The first board meeting of WWF approved a grant to the Charles Darwin Foundation's research station in the Galápagos Islands. This money was used to train Ecuadorian scientists in ecology on the islands where pioneer naturalist Charles Darwin had formulated his

The panda, emblem of WWF, has become the symbol of all species threatened with extinction. In 1979 the government of China invited Sir Peter Scott to visit their country and advise it on the conservation of the dwindling giant panda species. Eventually China set up ten panda reserves. Millions of dollars have been raised and invested in the panda project.

famous theories of natural selection. Galápagos fauna such as the giant tortoises and marine iguanas were also safeguarded.

WWF's first big conservation success came with the establishment of the Coto Donaña reserve, a coastal marshland and sand dune complex in southern Spain. Here, in western Europe's most significant wildlife refuge, the habitats of lynx, flamingos, and the Spanish imperial eagle as well as thousands of ducks and geese are protected.

One of the early campaigns to support a dwindling species was the struggle to save the Andean vicuña. The vicuña, a relative of the llama and the camel, was hunted for its silky fleece, and between 1945 and 1970 hunters in Argentina, Bolivia, Chile, and Peru had killed over 400 thousand vicuñas.

By 1970 only about ten thousand survived. Helping the vicuña was a long-term project. WWF contributed a total of $400,000 to antipoaching schemes and government plans for herd management. Vicuña numbers have increased to nearly eighty thousand. The goal is to establish a lasting trade in vicuña wool taken from the living animals.

A special experience

Peter's work for WWF involved him in worldwide travel, but one place he had always been reluctant to visit was the Antarctic. Although he never let the circumstances of his father's death weigh heavily on his spirits, somehow he had preferred to close his mind to the story of Captain Scott of the Antarctic. It was sad that he had never known this brave man.

By 1966, Peter was fifty-six years old. He was a celebrated artist, writer, communicator, naturalist, and conservationist, a world authority on wildfowl and many other aspects of wildlife.

He was a war hero, an international yachtsman, and a gliding champion. His own proven qualities of courage, leadership, and originality had made him a son that Captain Scott would certainly have been proud of. There was no longer any valid reason for him to avoid the Antarctic.

To the Pole

So in January 1966, Peter Scott agreed to accompany a film crew to Antarctica. In some ways he did not realize then that "the journey was going to be not only physically demanding but also emotionally stirring."

Peter wrote: "I think my most vivid memories will always be of my father's hut at Cape Evans, the base for his journey to the Pole in 1911-12."

Peter sat writing his diary in the very alcove where his father had recorded his own experiences.

His father had written, "Great God, this is an awful place!" Peter added, in agreement, "Awful because of its monotonous flat immensity . . .

"Awful perhaps because of Amundsen's tent, and being forestalled . . .

"Awful for the cold and the wind . . .

"Awful for the prospect of walking 800 miles . . ."

This striking photograph shows two male elephant seals fighting on the ice in Antarctica. Modern technology has made even this remote area open for development, and the seals themselves have been threatened by hunting and the effects of pollution. Peter Scott traveled all over the world backing conservation projects. When he was fifty-six, Peter Scott was invited to visit the Antarctic, where his famous father had died, and he decided to accept the invitation.

"Since then the place has altered little on the surface, but underneath is the snug warm camp with all its machinery. I wonder if . . . my father could have imagined flush toilets and computers [and] generators . . . under the snow at the Pole. Surely not. The circumstances have changed *too* much.

"A plane will take us in less than 3 hours to Hut Point. No gnawing doubts about the lateness of the season, no appalling disappointment at Amundsen's secretly changed plans, at his priority at the Pole, at the lost race, at the vanished daydreams. No dietetic problems with scurvy beginning to take its effect. No fears for personal survival.

"Yet . . . the Pole still has a magic and a majesty which can be felt. It is the South Pole. It is still there, just like Everest, even though both were conquered long since."

Five years later, Peter was to return to the scenes of his father's polar expedition. This time he was able to bring Philippa and Dafila with him. He confessed that he experienced "a great deal of pleasure in seeing my two darlings standing there."

An active life

Peter Scott was always active and energetic — he was not going to slow up as middle age approached. His oldest daughter, Nicola, married and Peter soon became a proud grandfather, but he continued to work tirelessly for the Wildfowl Trust, for IUCN, for WWF, and for several other conservation groups.

Much of his time was spent flying around the world supervising new conservation projects. He had to learn the art of delegation, trusting other people to carry out the details of his plans and projects.

By then, he explained, "I had learned two important maxims. . . . The first is: 'If you want work well done, select a busy man. The other kind has no time'; the second: 'If you want work well done, give it to an individual, never to a committee.' . . . I had long ago learned that no one in life is perfect, but one must be thankful if they do well what you want them to do; and if they do they must be praised, because almost everyone does their best work when they think they are doing well."

Wisdom like this meant that people were happy to work for Peter Scott, gladly giving their best in a cause they believed in. His staff has always been loyal, often protecting him from the inevitable demands brought by success and fame.

As he grew older, Peter Scott saw the start of new groups like Friends of the Earth and Greenpeace. He encouraged them as he came to realize that although different people and different groups had their own ways of going about the business of conservation, they all had the same ultimate aim of protecting the environment and maintaining the wonderful diversity of the world's wildlife.

The WWF presses on

As the time passed, WWF became responsible for a great variety of conservation activities. Three of the most famous were the fight to save the Arabian oryx

"According to his wife, there is seldom a moment when Sir Peter's thoughts are not focused on some aspect of natural history. 'If he has a one-hour layover at an airport,' says Lady Scott, 'he'll get a glass of water and do some watercolours of birds or fishes.' He carries a small paint set for just such an occasion."

The Christian
Science Monitor

49

Above left: The Arabian oryx, a symbol of the Flora and Fauna Preservation Society, an organization that cooperated with WWF and the Sultan of Oman in Operation Oryx, a successful attempt to capture and breed from the last few wild oryx.

Above right: A relative of the llama and the camel, the vicuña lives in the Andes. It almost perished because of demand for its silky fleece. WWF helped to save the vicuña by helping to manage the herds in the Pampas Galeras Reserve, where vicuña wool can be sheared without harming the animals.

from the brink of extinction, Project Tiger, and Polar Bear Rescue.

The oryx is an elegant and powerful antelope native to the Arabian Peninsula. Hunting had almost wiped out this beautiful animal, but thanks to WWF's cooperation with the Flora and Fauna Preservation Society and to Peter Scott's influence with the Sultan of Oman, a herd of oryx again roams the plains of Arabia. First, oryx were bred in captivity. Local tribesmen were specially trained to then gradually reintroduce the oryx to their native habitat. This complicated process shows the innovative conservation methods that Peter developed with WWF.

In 1971, the imagination of the world was captured by Project Tiger. The project was launched by WWF when a census revealed there were only 1,827 Bengal tigers left in the world. At the beginning of this century there had been about forty thousand. WWF raised and invested more than $600,000 while India's government raised several times more. There are now fifteen tiger preserves and, as an additional bonus, this project

Above: A magnificent tiger in the snows of its native Siberia. These mighty carnivores need large areas of land so they can roam and hunt. This can cause problems for local farmers.

Left: In Nepal a tigress is tended by WWF workers whose detailed studies are important for the survival of endangered species. Indian tigers thrive in forest reserves where vegetation is allowed to grow and protect them.

51

Above: Special postage stamps issued by the USSR celebrated its part in the international campaign to boost the population of polar bears.

has meant that once-denuded forests have been allowed to recover in India.

Indira Gandhi, at that time India's prime minister, was a great supporter of Project Tiger and of the conservation effort in general. Peter was in contact with her many times. "We need to put our ear to the ground," she said, "so that the Earth can whisper its secrets to us."

International cooperation was also vital for action to preserve the polar bear, or ice bear, as it is called in Norway. By 1973, overhunting had reduced the population of polar bears to just one thousand. IUCN and WWF persuaded five Arctic nations — Canada, the United States, Denmark, Norway, and the USSR — to sign the International Polar Bear Convention. This promoted scientific study and controlled hunting strictly so that within ten years the number of bears had doubled. A Soviet postage stamp was later issued to celebrate the recovery of the species.

Sir Peter

It was in 1973, the year of the polar bear campaign, that Peter Scott was knighted by Queen Elizabeth II and became "Sir" Peter Scott. In a certain way, this was not just official recognition of his great work and his achievements over many years but also an award for the entire cause of conservation.

No one had ever before been knighted for services to conservation. Care for wildlife and concern for the environment had "arrived" — it was part of everyone's experience. People knew that they had a responsibility for the Earth; they also knew that everyone could help conservation projects.

Recently, an English schoolboy wrote to Sir Peter, "My donation is not very much but it is all I have in my money box at the moment. I hope it will help the wild animals of the world, just a little, even if it only gives one trunkful of water to one elephant."

That child and millions like him would not have known about the problems of the natural world if Peter Scott had not spent so many years in filming, painting, and writing about animals and their habitats. Young Peter, the boy who had so disliked writing, was now the author of sixteen books and the illustrator of many more. Sales of his sought-after paintings supported his family and helped to finance his work. Everywhere he went, he sketched the wonderful creatures around him.

WWF grows

Throughout the 1980s, WWF worked on behalf of pandas, continuing to cooperate with the Chinese government. Gorillas, too, were safeguarded by a WWF project in Eastern Africa, and there were campaigns to conserve desert flora and fauna in Nigeria, where they were threatened by drought, the overuse of land, and hunting. Many educational and training schemes flourished as WWF spread worldwide, with national organizations on five continents. It is currently based in Switzerland and has over twenty associated national organizations.

In 1980, thirty-two countries launched national support for the World Conservation Strategy, a plan published by WWF, IUCN, and UNEP (the United Nations Environment Program). Peter Scott personally attended the national launches of the World Conservation Strategy in China and Hong Kong.

Forty-three countries openly pledged themselves to support the strategy's three aims: care for ecological processes and life-support systems (like the rain forests and coral reefs); the preservation of varied species (like the oryx, tiger, and polar bear); and careful management of useful natural products (like the vicuña wool).

WWF successes

Many successful tales can be told of species saved from extinction by WWF, such as the golden lion tamarin in Brazil and the St. Lucia parrot in the Caribbean. Numerous conservation areas have been established all over the world with WWF support, including Lake Nakuru in Kenya, the Annapurna Conservation Area in Nepal, and Peru's Manu National Park, six-thousand square miles (15,500 square km) of shelter for nearly ten percent of all bird species on Earth.

There were many more such encouraging stories,

"I rather exasperated Phil by going on painting my third caterpillar until the very last moment. Somehow I can never see why it is upsetting to go on doing things till the last moment. But I know that it is so, yet I was so very keen to get the pattern of that last caterpillar onto paper before we left and it seemed the only important thing at the time."

Sir Peter Scott,
Travel Diaries of a Naturalist

53

but the greatest success of all was the growth of the WWF itself from its humble beginnings in a one-room office back in 1961.

By 1986, twenty-five years after its founding, WWF could boast over a million supporters worldwide, connected through an international network with twenty-three national organizations and headed by Britain's Prince Philip as international president. WWF had sponsored more than four thousand projects in 130 countries and directed more than 100 million dollars into conservation activities.

Awards

The year 1986 was exciting for Sir Peter Scott. The boy who had never won prizes at school was given two of the world's most prestigious conservation awards. In Assisi, Italy, former home of the animals' patron, St. Francis, the WWF presented its Gold Medal to Scott, "the Patron Saint of Conservation."

In the same year, Sir Peter won the annual J. Paul Getty prize, an award of $50,000 given "for outstanding international achievement in the field of wildlife and habitat conservation." It is interesting to remember that but for Sir Peter's own work, probably no one would have thought of awarding such a prize!

Saving the whales

One of the long-running WWF projects with which Peter Scott was closely involved all through the 1970s and 1980s was the campaign to end the terrible exploitation of the world's whales by the few countries that still had whaling industries.

For over twenty years, Sir Peter had attended almost all the yearly meetings of the organization set up to control whaling, the International Whaling Commission (IWC). He sat through the week-long meetings — spending the time drawing birds and animals while he listened to the speeches — and used every opportunity to persuade the delegates that it was important to stop the killing that was so cruelly depleting one species after another of the great whales.

The IWC finally agreed that a moratorium on all

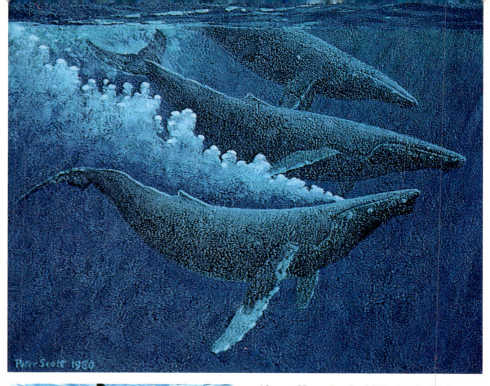

Above: Humpbacked Whales Bubbling, an oil by Scott. *In 1979 he and Philippa swam with a group of these whales off Hawaii. Scott wrote, "Humpbacks grow to more than forty feet long and can weigh up to forty-five tons. Throughout our meetings with them they were always absolutely gentle. . . . For both of us it was a totally unforgettable experience."* (Observations of Wildlife)

Left: A watercolor by Scott of white-bellied and Commerson's dolphins, observed on a voyage to the Falkland Islands off the coast of Argentina. "The star turn of the whole day for me were the dolphins," he recorded. "They were first seen coming in to our bow wave and surfing on it. . . . We must have seen a hundred or more." As always, Scott used his art to help publicize the need for protecting an endangered species.

"The part that my wife, Philippa, plays in my life is central. She is my principal adviser, she manages my business and financial affairs, she cooks my food and looks after me and the house. Although both of us have Scottish ancestry, she seems to have inherited more of the proverbial thrift of the Scots than I have, which at least counteracts my own tendencies to gross extravagance. Without her I'd be lost and bankrupt." (Peter Scott's tribute to his wife in the preface to Observations of Wildlife)

commercial whaling should start in 1985, but Japan, Iceland, and Norway continued whaling for several years longer by exploiting loopholes in the IWC regulations. This was one of several campaigns in which Peter and WWF worked closely with other international conservation organizations, such as Friends of the Earth and Greenpeace.

An appeal

In September 1986, Sir Peter Scott rose to address a huge audience of distinguished people in Washington, D.C., to express his thanks for the J. Paul Getty Prize. Characteristically, he did not confine his remarks to polite clichés, but spoke out boldly to defend whales:

"There is one particular and urgent conservation cause that I'd like to tell you about today. It's the desperate plight of the whales. A somber subject.

"Ever since whaling began, many hundreds of years ago, one species of whale after another has been hunted until there are too few left to be worth hunting. The pace of this destruction has increased enormously with twentieth-century technology. . . .

"By now, the Right Whale, the Bowhead, the Humpback, the Sperm, the Blue Whale, the Fin Whale, Bryde's Whale and the Sei Whale have all been hunted to the point of commercial extinction, and some of these species may never recover — ever."

Sir Peter went on to attack the prosperous countries that continued to kill whales. No doubt representatives of those very countries sat listening and perhaps felt suitably ashamed.

Sir Peter summed up his argument by saying, "The struggle to save the whales has become a symbol of the wider battle to save the many thousands of animals and plants threatened with extinction by the greed, cruelty and shortsightedness of our own species. That is why I'm still closely involved with bringing whaling to a halt, and why all conservationists need to stay tuned-in to this long-running struggle."

A year later, in 1987, Sir Peter made another attempt to shame the whale hunters. In 1971, Iceland had recognized his research into pink-footed geese by awarding him the Order of the Falcon, a medal which he now sent back to Reykjavik, Iceland, as a protest against Iceland's continued killing of whales. He said regretfully, "I really cannot keep it now. . . . I am dismayed by their disgraceful behavior."

Nations work together

Meanwhile, WWF continued to grow and to struggle for the conservation of animals, plants, and their habitats. In 1988, Britain's Duke of Edinburgh announced a change of name, though not of the familiar initials — WWF now stood for World Wide Fund for Nature. This was done for two reasons: first, the original English title was proving too difficult to translate into the many languages of the growing number of organizations in other nations and, second, the group wanted to highlight a change in emphasis in its work.

Increasingly, it has become clear, effort must be focused on the environment as a whole as well as on the fight to save individual species. The "web of ecology" has shown us that the destruction of wetlands or of the tropical rain forests affects the climate and wildlife of the whole planet.

Each day a vast area of rain forest is felled (to provide hamburger for U.S. fast-food restaurants, many people believe). The forest will one day be gone forever, together with the many species of plants and animals it sheltered. And with it will go a major source of oxygen for the Earth.

Rich nations and greedy people within the developing countries share the blame for much of this. Nations with money want to spend that money — on air conditioning, pleasure vehicles, electronic gadgetry, and other luxury items. Keeping a motorized and electronic culture going consumes natural resources and goods.

WWF wants everyone to know where their responsibility lies in this complicated situation. The world's poor have to think of today's wages and today's food for their children. They cannot afford to plan out the long-term effects of their hunting or farming methods. But people in rich nations, with more leisure time, can change so that their hunger for things does not destroy the natural resources on which we all depend.

"After many years of marriage I am still in love, I am still loved, I am still able to listen to music, and still able to do the things I like doing best — watching and painting and drawing wild nature, on land and in the sea. I still think I do not deserve such good luck, but not to recognize it, and rejoice in it, would be unforgivably churlish," Scott wrote in his seventies.

Happy years

Now almost eighty, Peter Scott lives happily at Slimbridge with Philippa. They enjoy frequent visits from their three children and seven grandchildren.

Peter is now an elderly man. He has come a long way from the days when, as a little boy, he had roamed the seashore with his mother and watched entranced as the geese flew overhead. The world, too, has changed radically from the time when Captain Robert Falcon Scott wrote his last message to his wife and son.

After a mild heart attack, Sir Peter has been persuaded to take life just a little more slowly. But he is still swimming forty lengths of his pool before breakfast, still lecturing, touring, writing and, of course, always painting.

With Philippa at his side and a devoted staff to organize his hectic schedule, he remains friendly and charming while accomplishing a formidable amount of work. Widely respected, his advice is heeded by conservationists worldwide, and few wealthy people or corporations can resist his gentle appeals for funds.

Perhaps the Wildfowl Trust, his first major conservation project, stays closest to his heart, and it is at Slimbridge, within sight of his beloved geese and swans, that he spends his happiest times. However far he might travel to promote the cause of ecology, the waterfowl of Slimbridge will always call him home.

Looking back over the past, he conveys two messages. One is about his life: "I am without question the luckiest, and I believe the happiest, man I know." The second is about his work: "I don't think we'll be able to save all we would like to save but I think we'll save a hell of a lot more than if we hadn't tried." Toward the end of a long life, he adds optimistically, "I haven't lost faith in the human species. I still think it has great potential for good."

It's up to us to prove him right.

Achievements of the World Wide Fund for Nature

Golden Lion Tamarin
This monkey is one of the world's most endangered species. A few hundred golden lion tamarins exist today, and WWF is partly to be thanked for that. WWF established protected areas for these monkeys and arranged for them to be bred in captivity. It then reintroduced the monkeys to their original habitat.

Gray Whale
Scientists estimate this whale's population to be between seven thousand and eleven thousand. It is in danger from ship traffic, pollution, oil drilling, and building in and around its breeding lagoons. With aid from governments and private experts, WWF developed a plan to save the gray whale — a plan that can also be used to save other whale species and migratory animals.

St. Lucia Parrot
During the 1950s there were about one thousand of these beautiful birds, found only on St. Lucia Island in the Caribbean. By the mid-1970s, the number had fallen to only one hundred. WWF helped establish a nature reserve and a program to teach people about the parrot and the environment. In 1980 the island's government passed a new law increasing penalties for killing, capturing, or smuggling the parrots, and St. Lucia's people made the effort a national campaign. As a result, the parrots are on the increase.

Vicuña
About 400 thousand vicuña were killed for their fur after World War II. By 1970, it was estimated there were only ten thousand vicuña left in South America. WWF's vicuña project established several programs to conserve the species. They bred vicuñas in captivity, started reserves for them to live in, watched over possible trading in vicuña, and educated the public. By 1980 the vicuña population had increased sevenfold.

Manu National Park, Peru
WWF has actively protected Peru's magnificent Manu National Park for almost twenty years, struggling to establish it and now working to maintain it. Almost ten percent of all the bird species on Earth can be found in its six-thousand square miles (15,540 sq km).

60

For More Information . . .

Organizations

The following organizations can provide you with more information about endangered animals and what people are doing to save them and their environment. When you write to them, be sure to tell them exactly what you would like to know. Include your name, address, and age in your letter.

Children of the Green Earth
P. O. Box 95219
Seattle, WA 98145

National Wildlife Federation
1412 16th Street NW
Washington, DC 20036

Greenpeace U.S.A.
1611 Connecticut Avenue NW
Washington, DC 20009

Sierra Club
730 Polk Street
San Francisco, CA 94109

National Council for
   Environmental Balance
4169 Westport Road
P. O. Box 7732
Louisville, KY 40207

World Wildlife Fund
1250 24th Street NW
Washington, DC 20037

Places to Visit

Listed below are some places that have been set aside and protected so you will have an opportunity to observe birds and animals in their natural environment.

Ocean and Shore Wildlife

Broken Group Island
Pacific Rim National Park
Ucluelet, British Columbia

Kouchibouguac National Park
Kouchibouguac, New Brunswick

Cape Cod
Outer Cape Cod, Massachusetts

Outer Banks
Cape Lookout, North Carolina

Padre Island, Texas

River Wildlife

Alligator River National
   Wildlife Refuge
Rodanth, North Carolina

Renewable Natural Resources Center
Bethesda, Maryland

Environmental Science Center
Houston, Texas

Riverbend Environmental
   Education Center
Gladwyne, Pennsylvania

Mississippi River Museum
   at Mud Island
Memphis, Tennessee

Unexpected Wildlife Refuge
Newfield, New Jersey

Wetlands Wildlife

Aransas National Wildlife Refuge
Austwell, Texas

Everglades National Park
South Florida

The Great Dismal Swamp
Suffolk, Virginia

Horicon National Wildlife Refuge
Mayville, Wisconsin

Mingo National Wildlife Refuge
Puzico, Missouri

Okefenokee Swamp National Wildlife
  Refuge
Folkston, Georgia

Tule Lake National Wildlife Refuge
Tulelake, California

Forest Wildlife

Allegheny National Forest
Northwest Pennsylvania

Big Cypress National Forest
Big Cypress, Florida

Big Thicket National Preserve
Texas

Denali National Preserve
Denali National Park, Alaska

Elk Island National Park
Alberta, Canada

Glacier National Park
British Columbia, Canada

Kluane National Park
Saskatchewan, Canada

Riding Mountain National Park
Manitoba, Canada

Books

These books will help you learn more about animals and efforts to save them and their environment. Check your local library or bookstore to see if they have them or if somebody there will order them for you.

All Wild Creatures Welcome: The Story of a Wildlife Rehabilitation Center. Curtis (Lodestar Books)
Clean Air — Clean Water for Tomorrow's World. Millard (Julian Messner)
Conservation from A to Z. Green (Oddo Publishing)
Earth's Resources. Radford (David & Charles)
Finding Out About Conservation. Bentley and Charlton (David & Charles)
The Garden as a Natural Reserve. Palmer (David & Charles)
Hazardous Substances: A Reference. Berger (Enslow)
Heroes of Conservation. Squire (Fleet)
It's Your Environment: Things to Think About, Things to Do. Environmental Action Coalition (Charles Scribner's Sons)
Lives at Stake: The Science and Politics of Environmental Health. Pringle (Macmillan)
Only Earth We Have. Pringle (Macmillan)
Pressures on the Countryside. Golland (David & Charles)

Rescue from Extinction. Brown (Dodd, Mead)
Tall Grass and Trouble. Sigford (Dillon)
Wild in the World. Donovan (Avon)
The Wilderness War: The Struggle to Preserve America's Wildlands. Weinstock
   (Julian Messner)

Magazines

The following organizations publish newsletters and magazines about the work they do
and about wildlife conservation. Check your library to see if they have these publications or write to the addresses listed below to get information about subscribing.

Audubon
National Audubon Society
950 Third Avenue
New York, NY 10022

Dolphin Log
The Cousteau Society
930 West 21st Street
Norfolk, VA 23517

ECO-News
Environmental Action Coalition
625 Broadway
New York, NY 10012

National Geographic
National Geographic Society, Dept. 00487
17th and M Streets NW
Washington, DC 20036

Glossary

Conservation
   The protection, preservation, and management of the environment and Earth's
   natural resources.

Coral
   A small animal that lives in colonies in the sea and has a hard outer skeleton.
   As the animals die, their skeletons form a deposit which, after thousands of years,
   builds into reefs or even whole islands.

Crustaceans
   A group of animals having a hard crust or shell, called an exoskeleton, in place
   of a backbone. They eat animal and vegetable garbage and vary in size from
   microscopic water fleas to the Japanese spider crab, with a leg spread of twelve
   feet (3.6 m). Crustaceans include lobsters, shrimp, and wood lice. Most live in
   the water.

Deforestation
   The result of cutting down forests either for sale or for fuel. The top soil is thus
   exposed to rain and is washed away. Finally, the area is reduced to scrubland,
   useless for either the original wildlife or for humans.

Ecology
   The study of the relationship between living organisms, such as plants, animals, and
   humans, and their environment.

Ecosystem
A community of organisms together with their environment. This can refer to a small area such as a coral reef or to a whole planet.

Environment
The surroundings of a living thing — such as a plant, animal, or human — that influence the way it behaves and develops.

Estuary
An inlet of the sea, especially where the tide meets the river's current in the mouth of the river.

Evolution
A theory of how a group of organisms such as a species may change, over time, so that their descendants differ in form, structure, and function from their ancestors. Charles Darwin developed this idea in the nineteenth century after visiting the Galápagos Islands, in the Pacific.

Fauna
All animals from the amoeba to the great apes. When we use the word *fauna* we are usually referring to the animals of a particular region or period. Often used in a phrase with the word *flora*.

Flora
All plant life from the simplest to the most complex. We usually use this word to refer to the plant life of a particular place or time. Often used in a phrase with the word *fauna*.

Galápagos Islands
A group of fifteen islands about six-hundred miles (960 km) west of Ecuador. Isolated from the mainland, they contain a separate ecosystem with many unique species of plants, insects, and animals. It was after his visit there in the 1830s that Charles Darwin published his theory of evolution.

Migration
The movement of a group of animals from one place to another. Usually, the timing of a migration is connected with the changing seasons. For example, many birds and some insects and animals spend their winters in a southern climate and their summers in a northern climate.

Mollusks
A group of soft-bodied animals without backbones. Many have hard shells or soft shells inside their bodies. All mollusks have a mantle, a thin layer of tissue that covers all or part of their bodies. In mollusks with shells, the mantle produces the shell. Mollusks include octopuses, mussels, snails, and slugs.

Pollution
Substances that enter our air, water, or land and make the natural environment dirty

or impure. The increasing pollution of our planet is one of the greatest problems facing us. In dumping waste from industries and our homes, we are poisoning not only the plants and animals around us but ourselves.

Rain forest

A dense forest found in the tropics where there is a lot of rain. The trees, evergreens with broad leaves, grow very tall. On the forest floor below are low shrubs and undergrowth. Rain forests are currently being felled at a rapid rate for farming and grazing of animals. Unfortunately, rain forest land is not fertile, so it quickly becomes useless for even this.

Reptiles

A group of cold-blooded animals with backbones and covered with scales or horny plates. They include lizards, snakes, tortoises, and dinosaurs.

Ringing

To catch a wild bird or animal and mark it with a rubber ring. This ring asks anyone who catches or kills the creature to contact the researcher who put on the ring. This enables the researcher to obtain much useful information, such as facts on migration patterns.

Scurvy

A disease caused by the lack of vitamin C. The symptoms include extreme weakness, bleeding under the skin, and spongy, bleeding gums. Anyone on a diet that does not include fresh vegetables may develop scurvy.

Species

All the animals of a specific type that can produce offspring. With animals, if no offspring result from mating, the two animals are probably from different species; any offspring that might result are likely to be sterile. For example, the male ass and female horse can mate and produce a mule, but the mule will be sterile, unable to produce offspring with either an ass or a horse.

Waders

Long-legged birds living near shallow water and feeding on fish and plankton.

Wetland

A lowland area such as a marsh or swamp. Birds often use it as a resting and feeding place during their migrations.

Chronology

1909   **September 14 —** Peter Scott born in London.

1912   **March 29 —** Peter's father, Captain Robert Scott, dies in Antarctica.

1917   The family moves to Paris where Scott's mother obtains a position in the British embassy.

1922	Peter's mother marries Edward Hilton Young. The family lives in London.
1927	Scott attends Trinity College, Cambridge University, England.
1930	**December 17** — Scott receives his degree. He then begins a year's study at the State Academy School in Munich, Germany, to learn to paint.
1931	Scott begins to study painting at the Royal Academy Schools in London. His studies there will last for two years.
1933	Scott sells his first painting. He leases East Lighthouse at Borough Fen and begins to sail in races.
1935	Scott publishes his first book, *Morning Flight*.
1936	Scott wins a bronze medal for sailing in the Olympic Games at Kiel, West Germany. He visits Hungary and sees the northward bird migrations.
1938	Scott travels to North America to paint and race.
1939	World War II begins. Scott enrolls in the Royal Naval Volunteer Supplementary Reserve. He becomes a First Lieutenant in 1940.
1941	British Navy adopts Scott's camouflage scheme and *Steam Gunboat (S.G.B.) #9* is assigned to Scott.
1942	Scott marries Jane Howard.
1943	Scott's daughter, Nicola Scott, is born. Scott sees action on the *Grey Goose* and is then assigned to teach on HMS *Bee*.
1944	Scott becomes Staff Officer Operations — Coastal Forces.
1945	Scott runs for Parliament but loses the election. He resumes painting and his study of birds. **December** — Scott begins plans for the Wildfowl Trust.
1946	Scott becomes commentator for "Nature Parliament," a children's radio program. **November 10**—The Severn Wildfowl Trust is officially formed "for the scientific study and conservation of wildfowl."
1947	Scott's mother, Kathleen, dies.
1950	Scott is elected to the Council of the London Zoo.
1951	**August 7** — Scott marries Philippa Talbot-Ponsonby.

He leads an expedition to Iceland to the breeding grounds of the pink-footed goose.

1952   Scott's daughter, Dafila, is born.

1953   Scott starts the British wildlife television series, "Look."

1954   Scott breaks the sailing speed record at Cowes. His son Falcon is born.

1956   Scott undertakes his first solo flight in a glider.
December — Peter and Philippa visit Australia and go skin-diving on the Great Barrier Reef.

1961   **September** — Scott helps to found the World Wildlife Fund.
He publishes his autobiography, *The Eye of the Wind.*

1962-80   Scott is Chairman of the Survival Service Commission of the International Union for the Conservation of Nature and Natural Resources (IUCN). He devises the Red Data Books.

1963   Scott becomes British gliding champion.

1966   **January** — Scott visits the Antarctic for the first time.

1973   Queen Elizabeth II knights Scott, calling attention to Scott's contributions to international conservation and to the conservation movement itself.

1974-84   Scott serves as chancellor of the University of Birmingham, England.

1980   The IUCN launches the World Conservation Strategy. This strategy is designed to help the IUCN decide which problems in the environment are most important. It also guides the IUCN in making suggestions to governments about ways to solve environmental problems.

1986   Scott wins the World Wildlife Fund Gold Medal and the J. Paul Getty Prize, conservation's most famous award.

1988   A new species of fish is named *Cirrhilabrus scottorum* after Sir Peter and Philippa Scott.

Index

Amundsen, Roald 5, 48
Antarctica 5, 47-49
Arctic 29, 32, 33, 36, 52

Barrie, Sir James (*Peter Pan*) 8
Borough Fen 17, 24

Cambridge University 12-13, 15
Canada 18, 33, 52
Caribbean 36, 53
Carson, Rachel (*Silent Spring*) 39

Edinburgh, Duke of 39, 42-43, 54, 57
Elizabeth II, Queen 39, 52
England 5, 8, 10, 16, 17

Friends of the Earth 49

Gandhi, Indira 52
Great Barrier Reef 36
Greenpeace 49

Hawaii 26-27
Howard, Elizabeth Jane 21
Huxley, Julian 42

Iceland 18, 33, 56, 57
India 27, 29, 51
International Polar Bear Convention 52
International Union for the Conservation of
    Nature and Natural Resources (IUCN)
    40-41, 49, 52, 53
International Waterfowl Research Bureau
    (IWRB) 28-29
International Whaling Commission (IWC)
    54-56

London (England) 8, 16, 19
London Zoo 8, 9

McMurdo Sound 5

Norway 52, 56

Olympics 20, 36

Pacific 36, 38
Peru 46, 53

Ramsar (Iran) 35
Red Data Books 40

Royal Academy Schools (London) 16, 17

Scott, Captain Robert Falcon 5, 6, 7, 8, 25,
    47-48, 58
Scott, Dafila 25, 32, 48
Scott, Kathleen 5, 7-8, 10, 17
Scott, Nicola 21, 49
Scott, Peter Markham
    as artist 9, 13, 15, 16-17, 19, 53; *Adven-
        tures Among Birds* 13; *Country Life*
        13; *Granta* 13; *Roof-climber's Guide
        to Trinity* 13
    as author 19, 39, 53; *Morning Flight* 17;
        Observations of Wildlife 39; *Wild
        Chorus* 19
    awards and prizes 39, 52, 54, 56-57; J. Paul
        Getty Prize 54, 56; Prince of Wales'
        Cup 35; Television Society Award 39
    birth and youth 5, 7-16
    education 10-13, 15, 16
    gliding 35
    hunting 14-15, 17-18, 24
    influence of his parents 5, 7-8, 17, 47-48
    and IUCN 40-41, 49, 53
    marriages 21, 25, 58
    military experience 20-21
    sailing 20, 35
    and Slimbridge 22-24, 27, 30-34, 43, 58
    and wildfowl 8, 11, 14-15, 17-18, 22-24,
        26-27, 29, 30-33
    and the Wildfowl Trust 22-24, 29, 33-35,
        50, 58
    and World Wildlife Fund 40-45, 49,
        53, 54-56
Scott (Talbot-Ponsonby), Philippa 25, 32, 36,
    49, 58
Scott, Richard Falcon 25
Severn Estuary 22, 24
Slimbridge 22-24, 27-34, 39, 42, 43, 58
South Pole 5, 7, 47-49

United States 18, 52

Wildfowl Trust 22-24, 26-29, 33-35, 49
World War II 20-21
World Wildlife Fund/World Wide Fund for
    Nature (WWF) 6, 41-47, 49, 50-52,
    53-56, 57

Young, Edward "Bill" Hilton 10